FOR
LIFE'S HARD MOMENTS

Thoughts & Prayers
When You Need Them Most

HOLLEY
GERTH

Promises from God for Life's Hard Moments; Thoughts & Prayers When You Need Them Most
Copyright © 2018 by Holley Gerth
First Edition, July 2018

Published by:

DaySpring
P.O. Box 1010
Siloam Springs, AR 72761
dayspring.com

Bible verses were taken from the following translations:

Written by Holley Gerth
Designed and Typeset by Heather Steck
Hand-lettered by Shelby Taylor
Printed in China
Prime: 71926
ISBN: 978-1-68408-217-9

Contents

Introduction

We live in a busy, broken world. Whether we're simply a bit tired or in the middle of a crisis, we all need a place to come and be still for a moment—a place to be reminded that we're loved, known, and supported. In my own life, I've discovered the promises of God to be that refuge.

He is our strength when we are weary, our hope when we are discouraged, and our encourager when the stresses of life bring us down. The following pages of Scripture, prayer, and thoughtfully collected content are personal invitations to approach God for whatever we need. You'll find, as I have, that His love is forever ready and waiting.

I hope this little book will be a gift for your heart. And I pray each time you read from it you'll experience the faithful care and loving presence of the God who is with us and for us in every moment, especially the hard ones.

Holley

acceptance

Therefore accept one another, just as Christ
also accepted you, to the glory of God.

ROMANS 15:7

God, we long for acceptance and are thankful You freely
and fully offer it to us. You open Your arms to us
just as we are and call us Your own.
Your presence is constant, and Your encouragement
grows us into all we're created to be. Help us to fully
embrace Your love and to pass it on to others.
Amen.

The world tells us we need to be "perfect." It heaps on the pressure. It tempts us to hustle for approval and praise. But I'm learning this: The breaks in our "perfect" facades are actually more like windows where people can most clearly see Jesus.

We do not need to have life all together. We just need to come together as we are.

We do not need to be flawless. We just need to be faithful and try again.

We do not need an "image." We just need a God who can transform us in ways beyond what we can imagine.

We are all a wild mix of beautiful and broken. Shattered and whole. Weak and strong. We are beloved daughters of a God who treasures us more than we know. He sees us as we are and graciously loves us still. Let's dare to do the same for ourselves and each other.

Anxiety

Cast all your anxiety on Him because He cares for you.

1 PETER 5:7 NIV

God, You are big enough to hold the world
in Your hands and loving enough to care about
the smallest details in our lives.
When we're anxious, You bring peace.
When we're afraid, You give courage.
When we're unsure, You provide confidence.
We release our concerns to You now
and entrust ourselves to Your love.
Amen.

I stand at the edge of a pond, ripples across the waters mirroring those of my unsettled heart. I pick up the rock the size of my palm and place it in my hand, running my fingers across the surface worn smooth by time and troubles.

I pull my elbow back as if I'm a human slingshot and throw the stone. It flies over the midnight-blue surface before skipping once, twice, and disappearing from view. I wipe the dust off my hands.

To "cast" our cares means more than just a tentative letting go—it's a hurling, tossing, complete release. This is the offer of God: to let Him take our anxieties as the lake takes our stones, fully and completely. There is enough room to hold one care or a thousand. We can let them all sink beneath the surface of His endlessly deep love.

This releasing isn't a one-time event. It's a lifelong process. We can come to the shore of God's faithful love again and again, as often as we need. Yes, we are always welcome to give Him whatever weighs us down so that we can continue our journey with freer, lighter hearts.

Brokenness

He heals the brokenhearted
and bandages their wounds.

PSALM 147:3

*God, You understand brokenness because You were
broken for us. You have experienced the pain
of piercing nails and heart-wrenching betrayal;
You are no stranger to how this world can shatter a heart.
You also know how to make what's broken whole again—
to bring healing and resurrection and redemption.
Please do that in and through us today.
Amen.*

As I drove home from work one day, the pain I felt seemed especially pointless, and in turn, my life did too. "God," I whispered, "how can you use me when I'm so broken?"

A song came on the radio that repeated a verse from Isaiah over and over again: "He was pierced for our transgressions, He was crushed for our iniquities; the punishment that brought us peace was on Him, and by His wounds we are healed" (Isaiah 53:5 NIV).

I started singing along with the words. As I did it seemed God whispered to my soul, "You think you have to take what's broken and make it perfect in order to be used by Me. But I think in a completely different way. I took what was perfect, My Son, and made Him broken so that you could be whole. And because you belong to Him, your brokenness can bring healing to others too."

It's a crazy, upside-down way of thinking. But it's true. God has used my brokenness in ways I never expected. It's become part of who I am, a surprisingly beautiful part. Like a mosaic, God has put my heart together again. He will do the same for yours.

You're Already Amazing

She believed she was

loved

& *it made her*

brave.

— HOLLEY GERTH

Burdens

Cast your burden on the LORD, and He will sustain you;
He will never allow the righteous to be shaken.

PSALM 55:22

God, nothing is too hard or heavy for You.
You are the load-lifter, the worry-carrier, the burden-taker.
Thank You that we don't have to sustain
all that weighs us down or hold ourselves together.
We release our burdens to You. And we remember
with grateful hearts that we have brothers and sisters
to come alongside us to be Your hands and feet
and help in our lives too.
Amen.

We all have times in our lives when what we are trying to carry through life is just too much for us to handle on our own. We're good at looking strong and trying to hide the fact that we're about to fall over. We wave away offers of assistance and plaster on a fake smile instead. But God did not intend for us to go through life that way. We need others to bear our burdens, especially when we're hurting. And amazingly, God Himself says that He will daily help us with them.

Somehow it's easy to confuse having a burden with being a burden. That leads to fear that we'll be too much for other people to bear. But the two are not the same. Your burdens are not your identity—they're temporary baggage. And when you let someone come alongside you and use their strength on your behalf, you're letting them love you. You're affirming their value in your life. You're saying that you trust them with something important to you.

It's okay to say, "I can't hold this up anymore. Can you please help me?" To do so is part of receiving and giving love. Whatever you're going through, you don't have to bear the full weight of it. God is ready and willing to bear your burdens so you can continue your journey. And He'll send others to help you too.

What Your Heart Needs for the Hard Days

Busyness

"Come to me, all of you who are weary
and burdened, and I will give you rest."

MATTHEW 11:28

*God, we still ourselves before You right now. Our every
breath, moment, day, even decade belong to You.
When our calendars are crowded and our to-do lists
too long, help us to choose what is best—
a life of love and trust and rest. Thank You for loving us,
not because of what we do, but because of who we are—
beloved children of the One who has given us
not only enough time but all of eternity.
Amen.*

Believing we can have it all, all the time is a myth and a lie and a joy stealer. What I do believe is that we can have God's best for us. A full life and life to the full are two very different things. One is about grasping, the other is about receiving. One is about cramming in, the other is about room to breathe. One is about striving, the other is about trust. One is about control, the other is about letting go— sometimes for a moment and sometimes for always.

On my bravest and truest days, this is my tiny manifesto for the begging calendar and needy to-do list and noisy-noisy Internet: I do not want to come to the end of life and say, "I didn't miss out on anything." What I'm aiming to say is, "I missed out on exactly the right things."

Fiercehearted

Change

We know that all things work together
for the good of those who love God,
who are called according to His purpose.

ROMANS 8:28

*God, change can be hard and painful. It makes us
feel unsettled and uncertain. In the middle of change,
thank You that You and Your promises are forever the same.
We know we can depend on You. You will see us through
and You will work for our good in whatever we face.
Even when we can't see or feel You, Your presence holds true.
Hold our hearts, hold our hands, as we walk
through change and into hope with You.
Amen.*

Some changes are far more welcome than others. But none of them is too difficult for God. And because He lives within you, there is no change too difficult for you either.

You have what it takes to thrive through change. Dare to open your arms and heart to what life brings. And know that for the parts that are painful, Someone Who Loves You has opened His arms to take the worst of that blow for you.

Jesus stretched out on a cross in the ultimate acceptance of change so that He could walk with you and give you life in the middle of everything that comes your way. He understands change is hard. He understands you may not want it. He understands you may wish your circumstances were different. He knows. And He knows you. He knows who you are now and who you are becoming—and He's committed to redeeming the changes, all of them, so that nothing is ever wasted in your life.

You're Going to Be Okay

God took care of me

Yesterday.

He's taking care of me

now.

He'll take care of me

tomorrow.

— HOLLEY GERTH

Comparison

I call to God Most High,
to God who fulfills His purpose for me.

PSALM 57:2

*God, it's so easy to look at others and wish we
could be more like them. But You only ask us to be
more like Jesus. Fix our eyes on You now. Focus our feet
on the path You have for our lives. When we're tempted
to look away or stray, draw us back to Your love
and purpose again, and remind us of who we are:
a one-of-a-kind creation made to bring You glory.*

Amen.

Before you took your first breath, God placed gifts within you. He wove you together with strengths, abilities, and that smile of yours that lights up a room. He made you irreplaceable.

There's one thing no other person in the world can do better than you, and that's simply being you. You are made in the image of God, and there's a part of who He is that only shows up in this world through you.

Not only did He form you before you were born, but He also made you a new creation when you gave your life to Jesus. Not simply a new person—a new creation. In other words, a completely unique being. Here's why that matters: if there's only one of something, it can't be compared.

You're not compared by God to anyone else, and that means you don't have to compare yourself to others either.

You're accepted, cherished, and even celebrated just as you are.

If We Could Have Coffee...

Condemnation

Who then will condemn us? No one—for Christ Jesus died for us and was raised to life for us, and He is sitting in the place of honor at God's right hand, pleading for us.

ROMANS 8:34 NLT

God, when the lies inside our minds get loud, help us to listen for the unending whisper of your grace. You tell us we are loved. You tell us we are forgiven. You tell us that we are Yours forever. Give us the courage to embrace the truth—Your truth— above all else, especially on the days when it's hard to feel it. You alone get the final say.

Amen.

If you could listen in on my thoughts about myself some days, it would sound like a series of accusations.

"You're not good enough."

"You need to try harder."

"You're just being selfish."

The harsh words we all hear in our hearts have many sources: our human self, the enemy of our souls, unkind people from our past. But we can be certain they are not from God.

We can silence them by saying, "I'm not going to believe or receive this because 'there is no condemnation for those who are in Christ Jesus'" (Romans 8:1).

We don't have to listen to the accusations. We don't have to live by the lies. We are not condemned—we are beloved daughters of a God who freely and fully offers us grace. He isn't our accuser; He is always and only our encourager.

Confusion

If you need wisdom, ask our generous God,
and He will give it to you.
He will not rebuke you for asking.

JAMES 1:5 NLT

God, You know **everything.** *The answer to every question.
The solution to every problem. The insights
for every circumstance. You promise to give us the wisdom
we need. So we come to You asking for eyes that see,
ears that hear, and hearts that follow Your ways.
Grant us understanding, and guide our every step.
Amen.*

God promises to give us the wisdom we need. All we have to do is ask and have the humility to receive the response, even if it's not what we expected. You have the God who knows absolutely everything living within you. And whoever you're praying for now is known by Him too. There's no problem too complex, no circumstance too confusing, no situation too overwhelming for Him. He's already got the answer. Even better, He is the answer.

Yes, there are times of waiting when we simply won't know what God has for us. But He does say that if any of us lacks wisdom, we should ask, and it will be given to us. We can ask on behalf of each other as well. Even though we may not know the answers, we can always come to the One who does and promises to share with us what we need to take the next step of faith.

The Encouragement Project

*S*ometimes we may not know

where we're going in this life,

but **we can always know**

Who will be with us

every step of the way~

the God who loves us.

— HOLLEY GERTH

Darkness

I have come as light into the world,
so that everyone who believes in Me
would not remain in darkness.

JOHN 12:46

*God, You have never been afraid of the dark
and You won't ever be. Instead You turn
the darkness into light. You have done so
from the very beginning of creation, and You
still bring light into each of our lives
and hearts today. We ask You to radiate
Your love where it's needed most.
Amen.*

God isn't afraid of the dark. He's not scared of the secret places in our hearts. The ones that haven't seen daylight for years. The kind with the locks on the doors.

God isn't afraid of the dark. He's not running scared from the tragedies in our lives. He is not backing away from the brokenness and the bitterness and the shattered dreams.

God isn't afraid of the dark. He's not avoiding the struggles or the addictions. He's not waving His hands in surrender to the enemies of our souls. He's not saying, "This is too much for Me."

God isn't afraid of the dark. In the beginning He spoke life-words into it and said, "Let there be light." Then He came as a baby into a midnight world and announced His arrival with a shining star. He conquered death in a dark tomb and rolled the stone away, making a way into the brightness for us all.

God isn't afraid of the dark. This means we don't ever have to be either. Even when we can't feel Him through the longest nights, right in the thick of it—He is always there.

Defeat

**Thanks be to God, who gives us the victory
through our Lord Jesus Christ!**

1 CORINTHIANS 15:57

*God, sometimes this life can be a battle. And in
certain moments it can seem as if we've been defeated.
Thank You that when we walk with You, defeat
isn't our destiny. We may get knocked down. We will
have scars. But that doesn't mean we've lost. In all our
setbacks and struggles, our wounds and wandering,
we are still more than conquerors because of You.
Give us the courage to get back up, to keep fighting,
and to claim the victory that is already ours.*

Amen.

When we have a weak moment, a bad day, a tough year, the enemy of our souls taunts us. "You've lost," he hisses. But that isn't true. The reality is, we can't lose.

Oh, we get knocked around in this life. We have bumps and bruises. Even our Savior left this world with scars. But that doesn't mean we're defeated. This matters because it changes how we fight. Imagine being a soldier who's going into battle. Your commander tells you, "We have already won. All you have to do today is go in there and obey my commands. Victory is sure." You would fight with less fear and more faith, less hesitancy and more certainty, less regret and more intensity. This is what's true of us. Even when the disease returns. Even when our spouse decides not to stay. Even when we relapse after promising we won't ever again.

Defeat is not your destiny. You belong to the One who overcame even death, and that means there is nothing too difficult for Him.

You're Going to Be Okay

Depression

When you go through deep waters, I will
be with you. When you go through rivers of difficulty,
you will not drown. When you walk through the fire
of oppression, you will not be burned up;
the flames will not consume you.

ISAIAH 43:2 NLT

*God, You have great compassion for us. You never condemn us
for our emotions or struggles. Instead You come alongside us
so we can overcome whatever we face, including depression.
Please give us the courage and wisdom to receive what we need
physically, mentally, emotionally, and spiritually.
Depression is only our current circumstance.
It can't change who You say we are or Your love for us.
Amen.*

Depression is real. And I believe we are whole beings who need help with every aspect of it—physical, emotional, mental, and spiritual. So if you're struggling with ongoing sadness, then learn the symptoms, go see your doctor, find a wise counselor, and do everything you can to help yourself get what you need.

Also know this: God doesn't condemn you for your feelings. Many of the well-known characters of the Bible struggled with periods of depression too. You're not alone in your struggle, and it's nothing to be ashamed of.

Depression is a hard enough battle on its own. God doesn't want you to add guilt and shame to what you're already trying to overcome. Instead He wants to encourage you. To encourage literally means "to give courage," and that's what God wants to do for you on the hard days. He says, "I'm here. I will help you. I will give you strength to take one more step."

What Your Heart Needs for the Hard Days

God will never leave or forsake us.

In our darkest moments,

our greatest trials,

even when we can't

feel His presence,

His love
is still
there.

— HOLLEY GERTH

Difficulties

"In this world you will have trouble.
But take heart! I have overcome the world."

JOHN 16:33 NIV

God, our difficulties aren't too difficult for You.
Our challenges aren't too challenging.
Our struggles aren't too strong. You live in us.
You are for us. You are with us always.
So even in our toughest moments we can have hope.
We can have strength.
We can take heart because nothing and no one
can ever take You from us.
Amen.

We can't completely avoid difficulties. In other words, we're not in control. While this is frustrating to hear at first, ultimately it can be freeing. Because if we're not in control, that means we don't have to live like everything depends on us. We don't have to make sure we're perfect so we won't get punished. We don't have to be afraid we won't be able to handle what happens. We don't have to work hard to keep God happy so we get what we want and the blessings keep coming.

Sometimes life's greatest gifts may even come from the hardest, most unexpected places. That's possible because "in all things God works for the good of those who love Him, who have been called according to His purpose" (Romans 8:28 NIV). Those words are not a hollow cliché. They're not a shallow way to comfort someone when we don't know what to say. They're a promise. They're our hope. They're the reason we can say, "God, I don't understand, but I'm still placing my life in Your hands today."

Do You Know You're Already Amazing?

Discouragement

Be strong and courageous. Do not be afraid;
do not be discouraged, for the LORD your God
will be with you wherever you go.

JOSHUA 1:9 NIV

*God, in this world we sometimes grow weary
and discouraged. In the moments when we want to give up,
fill us with Your strength to keep going.
When our eyes can't see the light, show us new hope.
When our hearts don't seem like they can take any more,
take all that weighs us down and lift us up with Your love.
Amen.*

I'm sitting in a coffee shop on an ordinary morning and my courage feels as drained as my latte, nothing but a bit of foam left at the bottom of my cup, nothing but a little hope left at the bottom of my heart.

We all get to this place as humans. It is part of living in this world. God knows this because He lived here too. He understands what it means to skin our knees, lose our grip on dreams, and want to hide under the covers.

I used to think success meant never growing weary. But I have come to understand it means not giving up. It doesn't mean feeling strong all the time; it's seeking God in our weakness. It's not looking as though we have it all together; it's knowing God alone holds us together. Success doesn't mean finishing first—it means taking one more step of obedience.

Battling discouragement doesn't mean we're failing—it means we're fighting. Even when we can't feel it, see it, or even imagine it, our victory is still sure. Not because of us or anything we do, but because of the undefeatable God who lives within us.

Distractions

Trust in the LORD with all your heart;
do not depend on your own understanding.
Seek His will in all you do,
and He will show you which path to take.

PROVERBS 3:5-6 NLT

God, there is so much in this world that wants our attention
and affections. Help us to guard our hearts from the
time-traps and temptations. Show us what's best and
give us the courage to release the rest. Free us from stress,
worry, and striving. We choose to love You above all else.
Amen.

This world will wear us out. The enemy of our souls would love to see us distracted by anything "good" that's not God's best. The people around us will always have expectations and demands. It's up to us to make a different, better choice. Scripture says, "I can do all things through Christ who strengthens me" (Philippians 4:13 NKJV). But it doesn't say we have to do it all. The God who created the world in seven days doesn't have any trouble with His to-do list. He didn't "hire" you like an employee to get work done. Instead He called you into a relationship of love with Him.

That means our work can be an act of worship. It means the solution to the pressure we feel to "do it all" isn't simply doing less. Instead, it's grasping on a much deeper level how much we're already loved. That's what keeps our hearts at the feet of Jesus wherever we are, whatever He may ask us to do.

Do You Know You're Already Amazing?

Doubt

If we are faithless, He remains faithful.

2 TIMOTHY 2:13

God, You said, "Come now, let us reason together"
(Isaiah 1:18 ESV). It's amazing that You invite us
to engage with you—to bring our questions, fears,
and uncertainty. You aren't threatened by any of those,
because You are God. You are the way, the truth,
and the life. So we humbly bring the challenges
our humanity carries, knowing You will give us
what we truly need most, whether it's answers
or the ability to dwell in the unknown.
Amen.

You may sometimes wonder why you have so many questions about your life; why it takes you a while to figure things out; why it takes time to decide on a specific path. There might be times you whisper to yourself, *Shouldn't I be more certain, more focused, more sure?*

From a different perspective these questions and hesitations are proof of a heart that delights God because you're pursuing truth and wisdom until you find it. It's evidence of a woman who's not afraid to ask the hard questions. It takes a particular kind of courage to be someone who can sit in the in-between until the next step is revealed.

Dear heart, keep seeking. See your questions not as a reason for guilt or insufficiency, but as evidence that you really want to know the truth. See your searching as a pursuit of the One who loves for you to chase hard after His heart. See your uncertainty as something that helps you search out the only One who is unchanging forever.

Keep walking toward Him.

Keep walking with Him.

Keep searching.

You'll always find what you're looking for in the end. Because you're really always looking for Him.

If We Could Have Coffee...

In every circumstance of our lives,

we still have the

same Savior.

The One who *loves* us.

The One who *knows* us.

The One whose *promises* never fail.

— HOLLEY GERTH

Expectations

You are not under the law, but under grace.

ROMANS 6:14

*God, it's so easy to live like we're under the law
again by trying to be perfect, earning Your approval,
and pleasing other people. When we take on
expectations You never intended, remind us
that life with You isn't about what we can do—
it's about what You've already done for us.
You are the heart-freer, the grace-bestower,
the chain-breaker. And we're so grateful.
Amen.*

To be women who live freely, we have to release ourselves and each other from expectations. They are prison bars God never intended for us.

In place of expectations, Jesus gives us invitations. He tells us, "Come to me, all you who are weary and burdened, and I will give you rest" (Matthew 11:28). And what burdens us more than expectations? God whispers to our hearts, "I know you can't ever live up to my standards. That's why I sent Jesus. You are free from striving. You can live in grace, and I will help you grow. I accept you as you are, and I will be with you as you joyfully become all I've created you to be."

When you feel a weight that's heavy on your shoulders, pause and ask, "Is this an expectation?" What's truly from God is not intended to weigh us down. We sabotage ourselves when we take on expectations because they're simply too much for us to carry. God invites us to trade those demands for the lightness of grace and real love instead.

You're Going to Be Okay

Failure

The LORD directs the steps of the godly.
He delights in every detail of their lives.
Though they stumble, they will never fall,
for the LORD holds them by the hand.

PSALM 37:23–24 NLT

*God, it's amazing that You hold us by the hand and never
let us fall. Thank You that You are bigger than our mistakes,
stronger than our weaknesses, greater than any of our
limitations. Our circumstances and struggles don't determine
our identity—only You do. And You say we are loved,
chosen, and more than conquerors through You.
Amen.*

The hill's steepness taunts me and tries to steal my breath. But what really tempts me to quit are the accusations that follow me: "You're failing. *This must be your worst run ever.*"

I used to believe doubts and discouraging thoughts like this until I discovered something: I would finish my "terrible" run only to discover my time had gotten faster.

Then I started looking closer at other times in my life when negative thoughts tried to trip me up, and I found the same principle applied.

We're not tired because we're failing; *we're tired because we're fighting.*

We're not weary because we're weak; *we're weary because we're winning a hard battle.*

We're not struggling because we're quitters; *we're struggling because we're refusing to give up.*

Let's recognize the strain and pain for what they are—signs of growth. In the place between what's comfortable and what feels like it may kill us is often where we become all we're created to be and to do. And You are with us every step, holding us by the hand.

Fear

"Do not fear, for I am with you; do not be afraid,
for I am your God. I will strengthen you; I will help you;
I will hold on to you with my righteous right hand."

ISAIAH 41:10

God, You are our Protector and Defender,
the Calmer of our racing hearts and knocking knees,
the Soother of our souls. Yes, sometimes fear will come,
but because of You it will not overcome.
You are our courage and confidence, our bravery
and strength, our peace even in the middle of battle.
Amen.

Fear is inevitable, but shame over it is optional. Fear is wired into our very brains, into the most primitive part of us. This is not a mistake on the part of our Maker. It is strategic so that we survive. God knows this, so He has compassion, not condemnation, toward our fear.

I have discovered that when God says "Do not fear" to someone in Scripture, it is almost always to someone who is *already* afraid. It is not a rebuke, but a reassurance.

Yes, as long as we are on this spinning earth we will experience fear. But it is not our identity. And we don't have to hold onto it. We are not people of fear. We are people of faith.

We are stronger than we know, braver than we feel, and loved more than we can even imagine.

We are *overcomers.*
We are more than
conquerors.

We are *stronger than we know*

and braver than we feel.

— HOLLEY GERTH

Feeling Invisible

LORD, you have searched me and known me.
You know when I sit down and when I stand up;
You understand my thoughts from far away. You observe
my travels and my rest; You are aware of all my ways.

PSALM 139:1–3

God, You are the One whose eyes are on everything.
You number the hairs on our heads, know the cares in
our hearts, and watch over every detail of our lives. We are
never out of Your sight. We are known and cared for in ways
beyond what we can imagine. On days when we feel small
and insignificant, help us to remember and rest in knowing
that You are with us, and that we're greatly loved by You.
Amen.

Maybe you're in a season of rocking babies or caring for aging parents or working on the big project in the office with the door closed. Maybe what you do feels invisible at times. If so, then I want to say, *"What's visible isn't more valuable."*

God sees us in the shadows of others who seem to be standing more in the spotlight, during the midnight hours meeting deadlines, and in the kitchen making scrambled eggs. God sees all that we do out of our loving hearts as beautiful and precious and worthwhile. The less-visible parts of life aren't second place; they are sacred space.

It's almost silent in my house this morning. The only noise I hear is the buzz of the fan above my head. It seems no one sees me right now. But God does, and He calls me beloved. He tells me that what I do matters. He reminds me I have a purpose and I don't have anything to prove.

Wherever you are right now, the same is true for you.

grief

All praise to God, the Father of our Lord Jesus Christ. God is our merciful Father and the source of all comfort. He comforts us in all our troubles so that we can comfort others. When they are troubled, we will be able to give them the same comfort God has given us.

2 CORINTHIANS 1:3–4 NLT

God, these may be some of the most heartbreaking and comforting words in all of Scripture: "Jesus wept" (John 11:35). You have tasted salty tears and know the sting of loss. You are tender toward our grief and gentle with our sorrow. Please hold us close to Your heart in our ache and give us hope that the hurt will not last forever. With You, "weeping may stay for the night, but rejoicing comes in the morning" (Psalm 30:5 NIV). Amen.

"Lord, if you had been here, my brother [Lazarus] would not have died!" (John 11:32).

Jesus doesn't offer answers to these broken-hearted words from His dear friend Mary. He doesn't try to dry her tears. He doesn't spout off a spiritual cliché. Instead He weeps along with her. The tears of a compassionate listener. The tears of a tender God. The tears of someone who understands the pain of death. Then He asks a simple question: "Where have you laid Him?" (John 11:34 NIV). He asks us the same.

He knows our hurt and He cries with us. He has not forgotten us. He will not leave us alone when we're in need. The Author of Life is still asking, "Where have you laid your Lazarus?" He's willing to go with us to the places of our pain. He doesn't fear what He might find. He isn't shocked by our emotions, questions, or even doubts.

Jesus grieves with us and then He gives us hope. He does come. And He does see. With eyes that stretch beyond humanity and into eternity.

Do You Know You're Already Amazing?

guilt

There is no condemnation
for those who belong to Christ Jesus.

ROMANS 8:1 NLT

*God, You say that all of us have fallen short
of Your glory (Romans 3:23). But You don't let us
stay in a state of sin. You lift us up with Your love
and grace. You fully and freely forgive us.
You release us from guilt, shame, and fear.
We ask forgiveness now for the ways we have
fallen short. We believe and thank You that We are
made right with You, not because of what we do,
but because of what You have done for us.
Amen.*

Here's what I've come to see: guilt is the modern-day version of trying to make sacrifices for sins. We mess up and tell ourselves we have to pay for it somehow. We sacrifice our joy, our worth, even our fellowship with God to show we are sorry. Then after we've done that for long enough, we feel as if we can move on because we have paid the price for what we've done.

Guilt is about the Old Testament law.

We are people of New Testament grace.

We don't have to sacrifice for our sins anymore. Instead, we can receive what Jesus has done for us. "If we confess our sins, He is faithful and just and will forgive us our sins and purify us from all unrighteousness" (1 John 1:9 NIV).

That's exactly why we need a Savior. Guilt and all our efforts that are motivated by it can never make us right in God's eyes. But the death of Jesus on the cross can. When we turn our lives over to Him, all our sins are forgiven. And when we mess up (and we will), we can receive more forgiveness.

As much as we need.

You're Going to Be Okay

No matter how today goes,
we can always try again
tomorrow.

*God's mercies
are new
every Morning*

because that's
how often we need them.

— HOLLEY GERTH

Hard Times

In all these things we are more than conquerors
through Him who loved us.

ROMANS 8:37 NIV

God, when hard times come it's easy to wonder
if we've done something wrong. But You tell us
that trouble in this world is inevitable—it's only
our response that's optional. We choose to cling
to what You say is greater than our circumstances:
Your love, faithfulness, and plan for our lives.
And we declare this: whatever comes against us,
You are still for us.
Amen.

Just because your circumstances are hard doesn't mean God's purpose for you has changed. Joseph, Esther, and even Jesus could have said, "I must have done something wrong. Look at what's happening to me! I'm going to give up and just hang on until heaven." Instead, each one looked past the present and held on to an eternal perspective.

You have not been sidelined.

You have not been disqualified.

You have not been placed on the bench to wait out the rest of the game.

God's purpose for you will prevail. In all of history, no person has ever been able to thwart God's ultimate plan. He isn't shocked by the brokenness of this world or even our personal failures. He can redeem and reroute as much as is needed to get us to the destination He has in mind.

You're Going to Be Okay

Heartbreak

The LORD is close to the brokenhearted;
He rescues those whose spirits are crushed.

PSALM 34:18 NLT

God, You see our tears. You know our hurts.
You understand our sorrows. In the moments when
it's hard to even put words to our ache, we ask You
to hear what we cannot say, to do what we cannot do,
to care for us when we are depleted, and to carry us
when we can't even move. Be our comfort
and our hope. Oh, how we need You now.
Amen.

The phone rings, the text comes, the email arrives, and suddenly your world is flipped upside down. Tears fill your eyes and your heart silently whispers, *"Where are You, God?"* And His answer is always the same: *"Right here with You."*

He's there in the disappointment. He's there in the darkness. He's there even when you can't feel Him. He understands what you're going through. *The hurt. The anger. The fear.* The not-knowing-what's-next. Your emotions aren't an affront to Him. After all, He created them. Instead your feelings bring forth His compassion.

Others may tell you to hang on, to hold it in, to just move forward. But the God who scattered stars into evening skies comes in the night of our souls and simply grieves with us. Whatever you're facing today, you're not alone. God is not waiting for you to get over it. Instead He's placing His love over you and longing to draw you close.

Impatience

I waited patiently for the LORD,
and He turned to me and heard my cry for help.

PSALM 40:1

*God, You have not forgotten us. You have not
overlooked our requests. You haven't left us behind.
Please give us the patience we need to wait for Your timing,
the faith we need to believe when we don't yet see,
and the trust we need to keep our hope burning strong.
Your intentions for us are good, and Your timing is best.
We surrender to Your will, not our own.
Amen.*

Patience requires giving up control, it means surrendering our perceived power. This is hard and scary for me. Yet, deep down, patience is also what our weary souls long for, what they are really hoping will be the outcome of all our efforts.

Patience isn't just about time, it's also about trust. It's about saying, "I don't have to be in control. I don't have to hold the power because I know the One who does. And He is for me. He is always working on my behalf. And this means I don't have to strive or reach for control."

This is the true work of patience—not only to help us wait but to help us worship. To empty our hands and bend our knees and bow our heads. This is a wild, heart-freeing thing. Because what we want even more than to be in control is to be cared for by Someone who truly loves us.

And we are. We always have been. We forever will be.

Our God is good,

and He loves us.

Even when we can't
see His hands,
even when we don't
understand His plans,
we can still

trust His heart.

— HOLLEY GERTH

Inadequacy

His divine power has given us
everything needed for life and godliness.

2 PETER 1:3 NRSV

God, You tell us the same power that resurrected Jesus
from the dead lives in us. The same power that spoke
the world into being. And the same power that heals
and restores and does the impossible. The truth is that we
are not all we need to be or able to do all You've called us to
on our own. But the even greater truth is, we are never
on our own. You are always with us, for us, and in us.
We are beyond adequate—we are filled
and empowered by an Almighty God.
Amen.

"Lord," I asked, "why do women feel as if they're not enough?"

It seemed I heard a whisper in response: *"Because they're not."*

For a moment I thought I had some holy static happening.

"Excuse me, God, it sounded like You said we're not enough. Could You repeat that, pretty please?"

Again, gently and firmly, "They are not enough."

By then I started thinking perhaps my heart had dialed the wrong number and the devil was on the line. But in that pause it seemed God finished the sentence: "They are not enough... In Me they are *so much more*."

As women, we're *much more* than pretty...we are wonderfully made.

We're *much more* than likeable...we are deeply loved.

We're *much more* than okay...we are daughters of the King.

I think the enemy tricks us into believing we are not enough because He knows if we discover the truth, we'll be unstoppable.

We're chosen, cherished, created women who have all we need to fulfill God's plans for our lives, and He has made us just as He wants us to be.

You're Already Amazing

Insecurity

The one who formed you says,
"Do not be afraid, for I have ransomed you.
I have called you by name; you are mine."

ISAIAH 43:1 NLT

*God, You are our creator and designer, life-giver
and purpose-imparter. You don't compare us
with anyone else, which means we don't have to either.
Give us the courage to walk in holy confidence
and be who we are, Your beloved daughters.
Amen.*

Eve circles the borders of Eden, never completely reclaiming the truth. She forgets her story. The people around her tell her different versions. The world is a web of lies, and she is the butterfly with paper wings struggling in the corner.

And all the while, the One who made her is calling her back, still walking in the garden of her heart in the cool of the day and saying, "I am with you." He offers what she longs for most—for Him to tell her who she really is, to whisper in her ear that He has made her funny and wise and strong and brave. That she is tender and resilient and complex and wonder-filled.

She is mystery and unveiling. She is salty tears and the sweat at the finish line, the lioness in the corner office, and lullabies in the night. She is not an afterthought; she has been an essential part of the plan all along.

Fiercehearted

Lies

You will know the truth,
and the truth will set you free.

JOHN 8:32

*God, we don't need more facts or information,
expertise or analytics. Because truth is more than
what we know in our heads—truth is a Person
we know in our hearts. When the lies get loud,
stir our spirits and draw us close to You so that
we can hear You above all else. We believe
what You say. We trust Your Word completely.
We are who You say we are.*
Amen.

Our battle against the lies our hearts believe goes all the way back to Eden. The enemy tempted Eve with the question, "Did God really say...?" That phrase is the tip on every sword of untruth. And the same enemy still uses it to pierce the deepest parts of who we are.

Did God really say you're loved?

Did God really say you're enough?

Did God really say He has a good plan for your life?

Before we know it, the lies slip in and our joy, peace, and sense of purpose slip out. But we don't have to live that way. We belong to a Savior who promised, "You will know the truth, and the truth will set you free" (John 8:32 NIV). How do we discover this truth? Through an intimate relationship with Jesus, the One who is "the way and the truth and the life" (John 14:6 NIV). Here's the secret: Truth is not just a fact we store in our heads. Truth is a Person we seek with our hearts.

We may have been wounded by lies, but we have not lost the battle. And we have been promised victory.

Do You Know You're Already Amazing?

We are dreamed up
in God's *heart,*
formed by His *hands,*

and placed

in this world

for a *purpose.*

—HOLLEY GERTH

Limitations

"My grace is sufficient for you,
for My power is made perfect in weakness."

2 CORINTHIANS 12:9 NIV

God, You are the only One who is limitless.
Thank You that You understand we as humans
are not and that You can accomplish Your
purposes through us anyway. The only kinds of
people You ever use are limited, imperfect ones,
because there is no other kind.
When we're weak, be strong in us.
When we're weary, be mighty on our behalf.
When we're losing a battle, be our victory.
Amen.

You are not a superhero. You are not invincible. You are intentionally human. You don't have to be afraid that your limitations will keep God from accomplishing what He wants to do through you. Even Jesus grew tired, got thirsty and hungry, and had other human limitations. What does that tell us? Being human is not a sin.

God can and will accomplish all He wants to do in and through you. Your limitations won't prevent that—but pushing yourself to the point of burnout just might. Take care of yourself. Respect what you need. Accept being human.

You're loved just as you are by a limitless God who can more than make up for whatever you lack. As Sara Frankl, an amazing woman who spent much of her life homebound and yet made a significant difference in this world, said, "There is such pressure to do everything to its limits, when all you need to do is do everything to your limit...to the limit God gives inside of you."

You're Made for a God-Sized Dream

Loneliness

God has said,
"Never will I leave you; never will I forsake you."

HEBREWS 13:5 NIV

*God, it's comforting to know that there will never be
a single moment when we are apart from You. When we
feel left out, remind us we're surrounded by Your love.
When we feel as though no one cares, remind us of Your
invitation to cast our cares on You. When it seems we
are overlooked or forgotten, help us remember Your eyes
are always on us, and that You know every detail
of our lives. We are never alone.*
Amen.

We all have moments when we feel alone. In a world where everyone seems to be connected, it seems ironic that studies show we're more isolated than ever before. That sense of separateness can create cracks that let lies slip into our hearts.

Lies that say, "Everyone has more friends than you."

Lies that taunt, "Maybe you don't really belong here."

Lies that even accuse, "If anyone really knew you, you wouldn't be loved the same."

Can we shudder together at the ugliness of those words? And then can we say as sisters that we won't listen to them anymore?

You are not alone. I am not alone. Even in the moments when we feel like we are. You do belong. You are wanted. You add value in ways no one else can.

If We Could Have Coffee...

Losing Heart

Therefore we do not lose heart.
Though outwardly we are wasting away,
yet inwardly we are being renewed day by day.

2 CORINTHIANS 4:16 NIV

*God, this world is hard on our hearts. Joy slips from our grasp,
contentment runs out the door, peace gets snatched away.
It sometimes seems as if we can never let our guard down
and simply rest. Please free us from this burden by being
our strength and the protector of the most tender parts of us.
When it feels as though we can't hold on any longer, hold us.
We want You to be the keeper of our hearts.
Amen.*

"We do not lose heart."

These words bring tears to my eyes, a lump to my throat. Because I am tired just now. Not so much in body, but in a deeper, invisible place. Yes, I, the one who sees the best in people, who reaches out in love, who keeps believing folks can change. This hope and confidence that is my norm has taken a beating lately.

As I lay in bed the other night, I talked to God about it. And through the darkness He whispered, *"I get it."*

And I suddenly realized He does. He really does. More than I can know, more than any of us comprehend. He knows what it is to love and love some more—to extend yourself so far that you are stretched out on a cross. And then to be rejected or dismissed or misunderstood.

Because this happens, the safest place for our hearts is not locked away in retreat, but entrusted to the One who, in the middle of all the noise and chaos and even danger, truly understands, protects, and brings restoration and healing for each new day.

god is still writing your story

It's not finished yet.
He alone holds the pen
that gets to write "The End."

— HOLLEY GERTH

mistakes

If we confess our sins to Him,
He is faithful and just to forgive us our sins
and to cleanse us from all wickedness.

1 JOHN 1:9 NLT

God, You are the only one who can turn
our mistakes into miracles—the miracles of grace.
The miracles of redemption. The miracles
of new beginnings. We give our shortcomings
and our sin, our failures and fears, our missteps
and mess-ups to You. Transform all of them into
true stories that give You glory.
Amen.

I think of my own journey of stumbles and falls, and there is plenty to give me pause. The words I wish I could take back. The choices I wish I could remake. The mistakes that, to this day, stand out like cracks in my favorite coffee cup. Just when I begin to feel downcast, God whispers to my heart, *"Sin happens. So did the cross."*

At that moment, it's as if the world stops spinning, time stands still, and I let out a breath that comes from the depths. It's full of relief. I decide I am done letting shame and guilt win. I am ready to let those moments go, ready to put the past in the shredder like yesterday's newspaper. I am choosing love. I am choosing grace. I am choosing to receive what has already been mine for so very long—I just haven't fully received it yet.

Jesus meant it when He said, "It is finished" (John 19:30) on the cross. He still means it today. The enemy of our hearts knows what God has accomplished cannot be undone. His great hope is to convince us that what we have done can't be either. But this is a lie.

The truth is, we are loved, scandalously and fully. We are forgiven, wholly and freely.

Opposition

**Do not be afraid of them;
the LORD your God Himself will fight for you.**
DEUTERONOMY 3:22 NIV

*God, You are for us so who can be against us?
Nothing and no one we will ever face is stronger,
more powerful, or wiser than You.
Please take this opposition and turn it into
an opportunity to show who You are,
to fulfill Your plans, and work everything together
for our good as only You can.
Amen.*

We all get to the place where we face opposition in God's will for our lives. Sometimes it comes from within—when the lies in our mind grow so loud, we're tempted to listen. Or perhaps critics and naysayers and committees on the outside do the opposing. Either way, the voices are loud and are difficult to tune out.

In those moments, it seems easiest and most natural to hang our heads and say, "That's it. I'm walking away. I've clearly messed this up." But, at the same time, perhaps Jesus is whispering, "Stay... a great door for effective work has opened to you, and there are many who oppose you" (see I Corinthians 16:9 NIV). He understands the struggle. After all, He faced opposition and resistance at every step.

Sometimes what looks like opposition turns out to be an opportunity. It's an indication that it's time to press in, press on, and refuse to give up. It's a message saying we are fighting a worthwhile battle. It's proof that we are making a difference.

Overwhelmed

Oh, Lord GOD! You yourself made the heavens and earth
by Your great power and with Your outstretched arm.
Nothing is too difficult for You!

JEREMIAH 32:17

God, You can do more than we can ask or imagine.
You have not faced a challenge too great, a mountain too high,
an obstacle too intimidating. When we feel overwhelmed,
remind us that You are Lord over everything.
You prevail through all situations, and You will see us through
whatever we're facing too. Act now on our behalf, and give us
strength beyond what we could ever have on our own.
Amen.

I think of all that's ahead in my life, then whisper these words, "I don't know if I can do this." I don't know if I have the strength. I don't know if I have the perseverance. I don't know if I have the wisdom. Have you ever felt that way too?

Thankfully, when Jesus said we could do all things through Him, He meant *this*... He meant the *right now* that stares in our faces.

What's comforting is, we don't have to be strong, because He says, "I will strengthen you and help you" (Isaiah 41:10 NIV).

We don't have to do anything alone, because He promises, "I will be with you... because I love you" (Isaiah 43:2, 4 NIV).

We don't have to figure everything out, because He assures us, "I will...teach you in the way you should go" (Psalm 32:8 NIV).

This is the secret that can empower us on days when we are overwhelmed: It's not about what we have in us, it's about *Who*. Nothing is impossible for God—which means with Him, nothing is impossible for us too.

Let's be kind to ourselves
and each other today.
Life isn't about perfection.

It's about *growth* and *connection.*

— HOLLEY GERTH

Perfectionism

For by one sacrifice He has made perfect forever
those who are being made holy.

HEBREWS 10:14 NIV

*God, You alone are perfect, and, through You, we have
mysteriously been made perfect too. This doesn't mean
we're without flaws or failures, but that we are whole
and complete. Perfecting ourselves is something
we can never do. It only happens through You.
When we're tempted to forget that and try to be good enough,
remind us of what You've already done
and who we already are in You.
Amen.*

Try to wrap your mind and heart around this: We are *positionally* perfect through what Jesus did on the cross for us, and we are in the *process* of being perfected throughout our lives.

The Hebrew word for "perfect" is different than our typical Western definition. It actually speaks more to the concept of being complete and how we are all we need to be in Christ. For example, an oak tree is the "perfection" of an acorn. So God's goal for our lives on earth is not that we are perfect, it's about *growth*.

So what's the difference between godly growth and our false idea of perfection?

Perfectionism is all or nothing.

Growth is little by little.

Perfectionism is all about the goal.

Growth is more about the journey.

Perfectionism is about outward appearances.

Growth is about what happens on the inside.

Perfectionism is about pleasing self.

Growth is about pleasing God.

Perfectionism is about what we do.

Growth is about who we're becoming.

Pressure

Grace to you and peace
from God our Father and the Lord Jesus Christ.

1 CORINTHIANS 1:3

*God, when Jesus was on earth, He was not about
performance; He was about people and fulfilling
Your purposes. When we feel as if we have to perform
a certain way or attain certain accomplishments,
bring us back to the truths that calm our hearts:
we are already loved. We are already accepted.
We are already chosen. Your yoke is still easy,
and Your burden is still light (Matthew 11:30).
Amen.*

Maybe I should do more.

Maybe I should try harder.

Maybe I should perform a little better.

Thoughts like these run through our minds, and in return we run through life feeling as though we aren't enough. What if we don't live up to our potential? Wouldn't that be the biggest waste?

And yet there is One who didn't live up to His potential.

He could have fed more hungry people.

He could have healed more of the sick.

He could have ended injustice once and for all.

Yet Jesus didn't. And He didn't reach the end of His life and say, "I didn't live up to my potential." Instead He said, "It is finished" (John 19:30).

In other words, "It was enough." You are not called to live up to your potential— to do as much as you can, as quickly as you can, for as many people as you can. (Hint: *potential* is usually just a code word for other people's expectations.) You are simply called to say yes to God. With all your heart. For the rest of your life. Until the day He says you are finished. And, yes, it will be enough.

If We Could Have Coffee...

Provision

God will supply all your needs
according to His riches in glory in Christ Jesus.

PHILIPPIANS 4:19

*God, You are our provider, the granter of our
desires and the meeter of our needs. You promise that
You will not withhold anything good from us
(Psalm 84:11). We ask with confidence knowing
You will answer our requests the way You know
to be truly the best, even when we don't understand
or the answer looks different than we planned.
Thank You for taking such good care of us.
Amen.*

God promises to provide for us. That doesn't mean we'll get everything we want. The timing may be different than we imagine. What we have in mind may not match God's plan. But He will take care of us—no matter what.

When answering prayer, God's part is to provide. Ours is to learn to be content in all circumstances as we wait (see Philippians 4:12–13). I love that the apostle Paul uses the word *learn* in that passage. Trust is a process. The more we discover who God is, the more we find that we can rely on Him to meet our needs. As we do, our striving is replaced with peace that passes understanding.

You are cared for more than you know, more than you see. So are the people in your life. You can be sure God knows all needs. And He already has a way and a plan to provide for each one.

The Encouragement Project

God
hears our
prayers.

He knows
the desires of
our hearts.

He understands
our deepest longings.
We will never be
overlooked or forgotten.

— HOLLEY GERTH

Rejection

Those the Father has given Me will come to Me,
and I will never reject them.

JOHN 6:37 NLT

*God, You are no stranger to rejection. You know
the sting of harsh words, the hurt of betrayal,
the feel of nails piercing the most tender parts
of who You are. Comfort us when we feel rejected too.
Soothe us with Your love. Protect us from bitterness.
Show us when it's time to wisely guard our hearts
and when we're to keep our arms stretched open wide—
just as You did when You died for us.*

Amen.

Whoever said "sticks and stones may break my bones, but words will never hurt me" must not have experienced childhood. Sentences slung at our souls wound deeply.

Some of my lies? "You're so ugly." "No one likes you." Ouch.

As I revisited those lies recently, I pictured God, with His hand over my heart, touching the places where those syllables still sting. And a passage from the Gospels came to mind (see John 8:1–11). A woman accused is brought to Jesus. The leaders are ready to stone her. But Jesus "stooped down and wrote in the dust with His finger" (John 8:6 NLT).

What Christ wrote in the dust is a mystery. But whatever it was, I know it was truth. And now we stand as women accused. The enemy is ready to throw stones at us. In the dust of our hearts, I picture Jesus writing truth that covers those accusing words:

Loved

Accepted

Chosen

Mine

Others may speak into our lives. But Jesus has the final say. He covers the lies with love. May He heal us and help us to believe.

You're Already Amazing

Sadness

You keep track of all my sorrows.
You have collected all my tears in your bottle.
You have recorded each one in your book.

PSALM 56:8 NLT

*God, You are tender toward our sorrows and
compassionate toward our cares. You notice
and value our tears. We need Your comfort
and encouragement right now, in this moment.
Please wrap Your arms around our hearts
and hold us close. Put our tears into Your bottle
and Your strength into our weary souls.*
Amen.

If you could read a record of your tears, what would it contain? You probably can't even remember each one you've shed or why. But it seems God does. David trusts that all of his tears are in God's record. Yes, God has a record. So, like Him, why do we write things down? Because we want to remember. Because they are important to us. Because they tell a story.

Perhaps all of these are reasons why God keeps our tears in His record. It's His way of telling us, "Your tears are not just water and salt to me. They are part of who you are. I value them because I love you." God gives attention to our tears. In doing so, He affirms that it's okay to cry. Yes, even the mascara-smearing, snot-dripping kind of cry. I think God sees extraordinary beauty in our ugly cries. That kind of crying is what it looks like when a human heart is laid bare and open. It's what we do when we stop trying so hard to be strong. It's our way of saying, "This is too much for me." It's—dare I say it—an act of worship because we finally let ourselves be humans who need God.

So go ahead and let loose when you need to, friend. Cry when you're sad. Cry when you're happy. Cry when you're angry. And I'll try to do the same, okay? Let's dare to tell the story of our lives through our tears, and remember that God, the Author of life, is treasuring each one.

What Your Heart Needs for the Hard Days

Self-Criticism

What then are we to say about these things?
If God is for us, who is against us?

ROMANS 8:31

*God, You are always and forever **for** us.*
You have the right to criticize and condemn us,
and yet You choose grace and mercy instead.
Help us to do the same for our own hearts,
which can be hardest of all.
Amen.

"If God is for us, who is against us?" (Romans 8:31). These words are meant to be a rhetorical question with the obvious answer being *no one*.

Yet it seems there is one other possible answer in my life—*me*. I can speak harsher words to myself than I ever would to someone I love. It took me a long time to see that doing this grieves God just as much as if I said them to someone else. When the critic gets loud, I can ask, "Would I say this to a sister in Christ?" If the answer is no, then my heart doesn't need to hear it either.

One of my favorite verses says, "David encouraged himself in the Lord" (1 Samuel 30:6 KJV). Yes, we are called to encourage others, but we can also be an encourager to ourselves. God is for us—that means we can be too.

Your past
is full of *grace.*

Your future
is full of
hope.

Your day
is full of
possibilty.

— HOLLEY GERTH

Sin

As far as the east is from the west,
so far has He removed
our transgressions from us.

PSALM 103:12 NIV

God, oh how sorry we are for our sin.
Please forgive us. We want to bring You joy
and to obey. Help us to truly change, protect us
from temptation, give us the strength
to choose what honors You in all we say
and do. This is our sincere desire.
Amen.

God keeps no record of wrongs. He doesn't have a file with your past in it. He's not racking up fines for you to pay when you get to the gates of glory.

When we deeply, genuinely believe we're forgiven, then we begin to respond from a new place. We have appreciation for the One who has canceled our debts, and we long to serve out of joy.

So if you've been worried that the hard times you're facing are simply because you "have to pay your dues," then you can let that burden go. God doesn't work that way with us. When He forgives us, He means it.

Today we can freely "approach God's throne of grace with confidence, so that we may receive mercy and find grace to help us in our time of need" (Hebrews 4:16 NIV).

What Your Heart Needs for the Hard Days

Striving

It is useless for you to work so hard from early morning until late at night, anxiously working for food to eat; for God gives rest to His loved ones.

PSALM 127:2 NLT

God, we wear ourselves out so easily. You alone offer the rest and reassurance we so desperately need. When we feel the need to strive, remind us that we aren't meant to work alone—we can draw from Your strength. When we keep trying to prove ourselves, help us to know that we already have Your approval—You love us the way we are. When we begin to listen to all the demands around us, call us back to Your peace and an awareness that Your presence is with us always.
Amen.

Instead of holding yourself together, can you let yourself be held by the One who loves you? He's the One who told the weary to come to Him. He's the One who tells us it's okay to lay our burdens down. He's the One who invites us to a life not of perfectionism, but of peace.

What do you need from God right now? Slow down for a moment and tell Him. Whisper the tiredness you feel. Tell Him about your frustration. Put words to your suspicion that the pressures are all too much and you're not enough.

Then listen for God's voice in return. Let Him reassure you that He's got you and He's never letting go. Let Him share with you that you are not responsible for results, only your obedience. Let Him free you from what weighs you down and instead lift you up with love.

If We Could Have Coffee...

Struggles

The righteous person may have many troubles,
but the LORD delivers him from them all.

PSALM 34:19 NIV

God, it's so easy to believe our struggles are our identities.
We can focus on the negative labels the enemy tries to impress
in our minds without even realizing it. Remind us
that struggles are what we go through, but who we are
is determined only by You. You say we are more than
conquerors, so give us new strength now to overcome
and turn our struggles into victories that fulfill the hope
in our hearts and testimonies that glorify You in the end.
Amen.

Stressed. Tired. Depressed. Anxious. Frustrated. Broken.

The labels stick to our hearts, covering our identities until we can't see who we are anymore. We come to believe that our struggles and circumstances define us. But those are just descriptions, not determinations. Who we are doesn't change based on the kind of day, week, or year we've had. We are daughters of God, holy princesses, women loved beyond all we can imagine. No matter what.

A friend going through a difficult time called me. As we talked, she kept repeating the same phrase: "I guess I'm just the girl who has this struggle." I finally stopped her and said as gently as I could, "That's where you're at right now. It's not who you are."

Your circumstances may change, but who you truly are remains forever the same. Your identity is eternally secure in Christ.

You're Going to Be Okay

We are not our biggest mistakes,

our greatest struggles,

or our worst moments.

We are beloved daughters of God.

— HOLLEY GERTH

Tiredness

God is our refuge and strength,
an ever-present help in trouble.

PSALM 46:1 NIV

God, You so lovingly built rest into our lives through
ways like sleep each night and a Sabbath each week.
Rest isn't a sign of weakness; it's a gift from Your
loving heart to ours. When we are tired, give us the
courage and wisdom to rest. Even in our busy moments
help up to rest on the inside, to release our worries
and burdens to You. May we treat rest as an act of
worship, a way of showing the world we know we are
not God and we are cared for by the One who is.
Amen.

It's okay to rest. It's even more than okay—it's essential.

I struggled with this for years until a friend gently laid her hand on my heart and whispered, "If you never get refilled, how will you be able to pour out?"

You are not infinite. You are human. You have limits. Acknowledging that is not selfish; it's worship. Rest says to God and to the rest of the world, "I know I'm not in charge. And I trust the One who is."

God doesn't need you to complete your to-do list. He created the world in seven days simply by speaking. He doesn't have any trouble getting things accomplished—with or without us. But what He has chosen for you and only you to be able to do is this: to love Him, those around you, and yourself. Part of loving well is resting well.

So pause, take a deep breath or even a nap if you dare, and in doing so, show the world that you serve One who is kind and loving to those who belong to Him.

If We Could Have Coffee...

Trials

**The Lord knows how
to rescue the godly from trials.**

2 PETER 2:9

*God, we don't like trials and going through
hard times. We want them to be over
as quickly as possible. Give us the patience
and perseverance to embrace where we are
right now. We also ask that You bring us
through this into a new place of hope
and joy that we can't even yet imagine.
Amen.*

One day I prayed, "Lord, I feel like I'm in a deep, dark cave right now." Of course, I didn't hear an audible response, but He did impress on my heart, "You may be in a cave but you have a choice: You can sit in the dark or you can diamond-mine your difficulties."

I decided then and there I wasn't leaving that cave empty-handed. I was going to take every blessing I could find with me. There were still many days when all I did was sit on the floor of the cave and grieve, but I also walked away from that time in my life with treasures I never would have found otherwise.

I'm discovering that the verse "Consider it a great joy, my brothers and sisters, whenever you experience various trials" (James 1:2) isn't a one-time thing. It's more of a process and a promise. It's something we'll be learning to do until we step into heaven.

Until then, we can know that with our God nothing is ever worthless, and hope can light the way to treasures we never imagined we could find in our hard times.

Unanswered Prayer

This is the confidence we have in approaching God:
that if we ask anything according to His will, He hears us.

1 JOHN 5:14 NIV

*God, sometimes it's hard to understand when You don't answer
our prayers in the way we want. When that happens, please give
us the trust we need to remember that You know what's best.
When answers are delayed, instill in us the patience to wait for
Your timing. When You say no, encourage us when our faith
seems frail and it's tempting to doubt Your goodness. We choose
to believe without seeing, to trust without knowing, to yield to
Your will even when it's a mystery.*

Amen.

Our prayers aren't always answered in the time or way we want. Sometimes God waits long past what we see as the deadline for action. When Lazarus became sick, Jesus delayed three more days before going to see him. By the time He arrived, Lazarus was gone. Martha, the sister of Lazarus, protested and said, "If you had been here, my brother wouldn't have died" (John 11:21). Yet when Jesus raised Lazarus from the dead, He revealed that He had already been listening and answering—just not in the way Mary or Martha expected. We live in a fallen world, so some answers may not come this side of heaven. But God promises that one day we will understand.

In our everyday lives, we wait and pray for lots of things—positive job interviews, good test results, mended relationships, or other breakthroughs. And even when we seem to hear nothing at all—when the house is getting colder and the danger is increasing—we can be sure God knows and cares. Silence isn't the absence of God hearing, but rather the sound of Him listening.

Coffee for Your Heart

God

pays attention

to every detail of our lives.

*He numbers the hairs
on our heads.
He knows the cares
in our hearts.*

— HOLLEY GERTH

Uncertainty about the Future

Surely Your goodness and love will follow me
all the days of my life,
and I will dwell in the house of the LORD forever.

PSALM 23:6 NIV

God, You tell us we don't have to worry about tomorrow.
That's not because hard things won't ever come,
but because You will always be with us when they do.
You are our security, our hope, and our future.
No matter what happens, You will take care of us.
You always have, You always will.

Amen.

Our future is secure not in circumstances, but in a Person—in

a God who loves you;

a God who holds the world in His hands;

a God who gave His Son for you;

a God who does not change.

We don't escape heartache and trouble in this life. But we do have the promise that this isn't the end of our story. God is working out His plan for us, and nothing can stop Him. That means what's most certain about our future is God himself.

When nothing makes sense, when all our expectations fall short, when our plans get derailed, there is only One who can offer us a firm foundation for whatever is ahead. When we place our lives in God's hands, our future is secure.

You're Going to Be Okay

Waiting

Many are the plans in a person's heart,
but it is the LORD's purpose that prevails.

PROVERBS 19:21 NIV

*God, we look at the hands of time and so often want them
to hurry. When we're tempted to do so, help us to look at
Your hands in our lives and trust Your plan instead.
We see only the here and now, but You understand all
of eternity. Even when we can't see what You're doing,
You are working for our good and Your glory. Sustain us
in the waiting, give us the strength not to jump ahead of You.
We wait with anticipation of seeing what You will do.
Amen.*

While you're waiting, God is working. Even before you spoke your first prayer, He had already begun His work in you. While you are going through each day and sleeping through the night, He is turning His purposes into reality.

It's hard when you don't see what God is doing or know when the time will come for His work to become clear. Yet that's what faith means—to believe without sight...to wait, trust, and keep watching. God understands that this is difficult. He doesn't condemn you for wanting things to happen now. Instead, He offers all you need to press on for each day.

A delay doesn't mean you've taken a detour. It doesn't mean a closed door. It simply means that your ways are not like God's. The eternal One isn't limited by time the way you are. He has heard you. He still hears you. And He is listening with love.

You have not been overlooked, forgotten, or set aside for something more important. No, my friend, every detail of your circumstance is in His care. You're never out of His thoughts, never out of His plans. Not for one day. Not for one moment. Not even for a second.

If We Could Have Coffee

Wasted Time

He has made everything beautiful in its time.

ECCLESIASTES 3:11 ESV

God, we can feel so much pressure to strive in every moment we have on earth so that we can prove our worth. When we're in seasons of waiting, take a detour, or things don't move as fast as we hope, we get discouraged. Yet there are so many times in Your plan when what looks like "wasted time" was actually necessary for preparation or part of Your perfect purpose. Jesus being a carpenter, Moses in the desert, Sarah not becoming pregnant until late in her life—all are examples of You working in the delays. Instead of driving each moment to rush a result, help us to trust that You are making each moment what You want it to be.

Amen.

Sometimes what we see as wasted time is actually the training ground for what God has in store for us. The lessons we learn and the obstacles we overcome equip us for growth and prepare us for how God wants to use us next. Even the rocks you're struggling to climb today are the stepping-stones of your tomorrow. God never wastes anything. There is great value in where He has led you. And even if you have strayed from His path at times, He's a Redeemer who can transform those mistakes into future benefits to you as well.

Right now you may feel frustrated or heartbroken. But God won't let this hurt or hard time go unused. He is working, even now, to use all of your circumstances in ways you can't yet see. With Him it's not wasted time; in His redeeming hands it's a precious bit of eternity.

God gets the final word
on who we are.

And He says we are

*beloved
and
chosen,*

cherished
and
gifted.

— HOLLEY GERTH

Weakness

He gives power and strength to His people.

PSALM 68:35 NRSV

God, thank You for choosing to use us
as we are and empowering us to be all we need
for Your purposes. Thank You that we don't
have to be strong enough— we only need to rely
on You. You use our weaknesses in ways
we can't even imagine. So we surrender them
to You now and ask You to transform them
into ways that show Your glory.
Amen.

Your weaknesses and struggles are not reasons for God to give up on you. Instead, they're opportunities for you to show His strength in ways you simply can't, even on your best days. The apostle Paul wrestled with a "thorn in his flesh" (see 2 Corinthians 12:7). We don't know what the thorn was exactly, only that it was an ongoing source of difficulty for him. He begged God to take it away, and many of us are familiar with the divine response. God said, "My strength is made perfect in weakness" (2 Corinthians 12:9 NKJV). In other words, the very places and times when you feel God can use you least are when He may actually shine through you most.

Here is why you are irreplaceable: because you are made in the image of the God who created the universe, and there is a part of who He is that gets shown only through who you are. Sometimes that happens through our strengths. But sometimes it's through our cracks that His light shines the brightest.

You're Going to Be Okay

Weariness

Those who hope in the LORD will renew their strength.
They will soar on wings like eagles; they will run
and not grow weary, they will walk and not be faint.

ISAIAH 40:31 NIV

*God, You understand that we are human. Sometimes
we grow tired. Sometimes our hearts are weary.
Sometimes we feel as if we don't have the strength to take
another step. Thank You that we can come to You in those
times without shame, fear, or guilt. Give us the confidence
to do so now—to rest in Your arms, to receive Your strength,
to let You restore us in every way that we need.*
Amen.

We serve a God who napped on a boat in the middle of a storm (Luke 8)... Who sent an angel to feed the prophet Elijah and let him rest after an epic spiritual victory (1 Kings 19)... Who calls Himself a Shepherd and leads us by still waters and makes us lie down in green pastures (Psalm 23). He is not unfamiliar with our human limitations or with our need for sleep and food and quiet.

When we are weary, it's not a time to be ashamed. It's simply a call to come in from the battlefield for a while—to safety and encouragement and a good, hot meal. Weariness is the deepest part of who we are telling us, "Well done. You have fought long enough for now."

Listen closely: Heeding this is just as much obedience as answering the call to the fight in the first place. Someone once said to me, "Rest is your sacred duty." There is a time for battle, but there is also a time to stay, wait, heal, and recover.

This is not weakness; it is worship.

Worry

"Therefore I tell you, do not worry about your life....
Look at the birds of the air; they do not sow or reap
or store away in barns, and yet your heavenly Father
feeds them. Are you not much more valuable than they?
...But seek first His kingdom and His righteousness,
and all these things will be given to you as well."

MATTHEW 6:25–26, 33 NIV

*God, You understand our humanity, how we are prone to worry
and fear, and how we stare at the ceiling in the night and focus
on burdens we are carrying. You've been where we are,
You've walked in our shoes. Help us to take You at Your word
and lean into Your love. Help us replace our worry with trust,
our striving with rest, and our pressures with Your peace.
Amen.*

Into the place of fear there comes a God-whisper, *"Your worry cannot change your circumstances, only I can."*

Isn't that what we really want to know? That someone is taking care of us, of others, of the situation, of the thing that makes our pillow soaked with salty tears. This is what God says He will do: He will look out for the sparrows with their wispy feathers and fragile bones, and He will look out for us too, with our tender hearts and glass lives.

And even when the worst of events comes, when everything shatters, God can make it (and us) whole again. *What frees our hearts isn't worry; it's worship.* In other words, taking all the hard things to Someone who cares. Choosing to trust and surrender. Believing His promises through our blood, sweat, and tears.

Here's what we can rest in today: the only One who has ever been able to bear the weight of the world is strong and loving enough to carry all that concerns us too.

ACKNOWLEDGMENTS

Special thanks to Revell, a division of Baker Publishing Group, for permission to include content from Holley Gerth's books in Promises from God for Life's Hard Moments. *To find all of Holley's books, visit your favorite book retailer, dayspring.com or holleygerth.com.*

Brokenness: Gerth, Holley. *You're Already Amazing: Embracing Who You Are, Becoming All God Created You to Be.* Michigan: Revell, 2012. Kindle.

Burdens: Gerth, Holley. *What Your Heart Needs for the Hard Days: 52 Encouraging Truths to Hold On To.* Michigan: Revell, 2014. Kindle.

Busyness: Gerth, Holley. *Fiercehearted: Live Fully, Love Bravely.* Michigan: Revell, 2017. Kindle.

Change: Gerth, Holley. *You're Going to Be Okay: Encouraging Truth Your Heart Needs to Hear, Especially on the Hard Days.* Michigan: Revell, 2014. Kindle.

Comparison: Gerth, Holley. *If We Could Have Coffee...* (E-book Shorts): *30 Days of Heart-to-Heart Encouragement.* Michigan: Revell, 2014. Kindle.

Confusion: Gerth, Holley. *The Encouragement Project* (E-book Shorts): *21 Heart-to-Heart Ways to Show You Care.* Michigan: Revell, 2015. Kindle.

Defeat: Gerth, Holley. *You're Going to Be Okay: Encouraging Truth Your Heart Needs to Hear, Especially on the Hard Days.* Michigan: Revell, 2014. Kindle.

Depression: Gerth, Holley. *What Your Heart Needs for the Hard Days: 52 Encouraging Truths to Hold On To.* Michigan: Revell, 2014. Kindle.

Difficulties: Gerth, Holley. *Do You Know You're Already Amazing?: 30 Truths to Set Your Heart Free.* Michigan: Revell, 2016. Kindle.

Distractions: Gerth, Holley. *Do You Know You're Already Amazing?: 30 Truths to Set Your Heart Free.* Michigan: Revell, 2016. Kindle.

Doubt: Gerth, Holley. *If We Could Have Coffee...* (E-book Shorts): *30 Days of Heart-to-Heart Encouragement.* Michigan: Revell, 2014. Kindle.

Expectations: Gerth, Holley. *You're Going to Be Okay: Encouraging Truth Your Heart Needs to Hear, Especially on the Hard Days.* Michigan: Revell, 2014. Kindle.

Grief: Gerth, Holley. *Do You Know You're Already Amazing?: 30 Truths to Set Your Heart Free.* Michigan: Revell, 2016. Kindle.

Hard Times: Gerth, Holley. *You're Going to Be Okay: Encouraging Truth Your Heart Needs to Hear, Especially on the Hard Days.* Michigan: Revell, 2014. Kindle.

Inadequacy: Gerth, Holley. *Do You Know You're Already Amazing?: 30 Truths to Set Your Heart Free.* Michigan: Revell, 2016. Kindle.

Lies: Gerth, Holley. *Do You Know You're Already Amazing?: 30 Truths to Set Your Heart Free.* Michigan: Revell, 2016. Kindle.

Limitations: Gerth, Holley. *You're Made for a God-Sized Dream: Opening the Door to All God Has for You.* Michigan: Revell, 2013. Kindle.

Loneliness: Gerth, Holley. *If We Could Have Coffee...* (E-book Shorts): *30 Days of Heart-to-Heart Encouragement.* Michigan: Revell, 2014. Kindle.

Pressure: Gerth, Holley. *If We Could Have Coffee...* (E-book Shorts): *30 Days of Heart-to-Heart Encouragement.* Michigan: Revell, 2014. Kindle.

Provision: Gerth, Holley. *The Encouragement Project* (E-book Shorts): *21 Heart-to-Heart Ways to Show You Care.* Michigan: Revell, 2015. Kindle.

Rejection: Gerth, Holley. *You're Already Amazing: Embracing Who You Are, Becoming All God Created You to Be.* Michigan: Revell, 2012. Kindle.

Sadness: Gerth, Holley. *What Your Heart Needs for the Hard Days: 52 Encouraging Truths to Hold On To.* Michigan: Revell, 2014. Kindle.

Sin: Gerth, Holley. *What Your Heart Needs for the Hard Days: 52 Encouraging Truths to Hold On To.* Michigan: Revell, 2014. Kindle.

Striving: Gerth, Holley. *If We Could Have Coffee...* (E-book Shorts): *30 Days of Heart-to-Heart Encouragement.* Michigan: Revell, 2014. Kindle.

Struggles: Gerth, Holley. *You're Going to Be Okay: Encouraging Truth Your Heart Needs to Hear, Especially on the Hard Days.* Michigan: Revell, 2014. Kindle.

Tiredness: Gerth, Holley. *If We Could Have Coffee...* (E-book Shorts): *30 Days of Heart-to-Heart Encouragement.* Michigan: Revell, 2014. Kindle.

Prayer: Gerth, Holley. *Coffee for Your Heart: 40 Mornings of Life-Changing Encouragement.* Oregon: Harvest House, 2017. Kindle.

Uncertainty about the Future: Gerth, Holley. *You're Going to Be Okay: Encouraging Truth Your Heart Needs to Hear, Especially on the Hard Days.* Michigan: Revell, 2014. Kindle.

Waiting: Gerth, Holley. *If We Could Have Coffee...* (E-book Shorts): *30 Days of Heart-to-Heart Encouragement.* Michigan: Revell, 2014. Kindle.

Weakness: Gerth, Holley. *You're Going to Be Okay: Encouraging Truth Your Heart Needs to Hear, Especially on the Hard Days.* Michigan: Revell, 2014. Kindle.

LIVE YOUR FAITH

Dear Friend,

This book was prayerfully crafted with you, the reader, in mind—every word, every sentence, every page—was thoughtfully written, designed, and packaged to encourage you...right where you are this very moment. At DaySpring, our vision is to see every person experience the life-changing message of God's love. So, as we worked through rough drafts, design changes, edits and details, we prayed for you to deeply experience His unfailing love, indescribable peace, and pure joy. It is our sincere hope that through these Truth-filled pages your heart will be blessed, knowing that God cares about you—your desires and disappointments, your challenges and dreams.

He knows. He cares. He loves you unconditionally.

BLESSINGS!
THE DAYSPRING BOOK TEAM

Additional copies of this book and
other DaySpring titles can be purchased
at fine bookstores everywhere.
Order online at dayspring.com
or
by phone at 1-877-751-4347